We the People

The Monongah Mining Disaster

by Jason Skog

Content Adviser: Paul H. Rakes, Ph.D.,
Department of History,
West Virginia University Institute of Technology

Reading Adviser: Rosemary G. Palmer, Ph.D.,
Department of Literacy,
College of Education, Boise State University

Compass Point Books · Minneapolis, Minnesota

Compass Point Books
3109 West 50th Street, #115
Minneapolis, MN 55410

On the cover: Aftermath of Monongah mining disaster, mine No. 8.

Photographs ©: West Virginia State Archives, cover, 27; Prints Old and Rare, back cover (far left); Library of Congress, back cover, 4, 8, 10, 12, 13, 25, 35, 37, 38; West Virginia and Regional History Collection, West Virginia University Libraries, 6, 14, 16, 18, 20, 22, 29, 30, 32, 33; Mine Safety and Health Administration, U.S. Department of Labor, 26; AP Photo/Jeff Gentner, 39; Christine Martin, 41.

This book was manufactured with paper containing at least 10 percent post-consumer waste.

Editor: Julie Gassman
Page Production: Lori Bye
Photo Researcher: Svetlana Zhurkin
Cartographer: XNR Productions, Inc.
Library Consultant: Kathleen Baxter

Creative Director: Keith Griffin
Editorial Director: Nick Healy
Managing Editor: Catherine Neitge

Library of Congress Cataloging-in-Publication Data
Skog, Jason.
The Monongah mining disaster / by Jason Skog; content adviser, Paul H. Rakes.
p. cm. — (We the people)
Includes index.
ISBN 978-0-7565-3513-1 (library binding) 1. Monongah Mines Disaster, Monongah, W. Va., 1907. I. Title. II. Series.
TN313.S56 2008
363.11'9622330975454—dc22 2007033107

Visit Compass Point Books on the Internet at *www.compasspointbooks.com*
or e-mail your request to *custserv@compasspointbooks.com*

Table of Contents

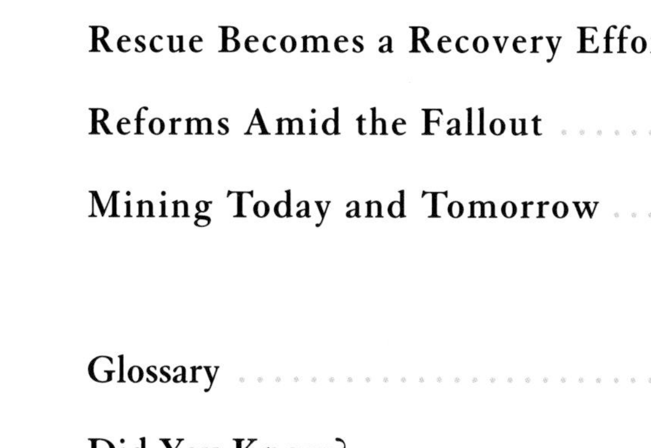

The Monongah Mining Disaster • The Monongah Mining Disaster

Disaster Strikes

On the quiet morning of December 6, 1907, hundreds of Monongah, West Virginia, wives kissed their husbands goodbye. It was considered bad luck for a miner's wife not to kiss her husband before he left for work. Death and

Coal mining has been a major industry in West Virginia since the mid-1800s. The fossil fuel is found in 53 of West Virginia's 55 counties.

injuries were common concerns in mining. Wives often worried it would be the last time they would see their husbands. With pickaxes slung over their shoulders and lunch pails in their hands, the men set off for work. They had no idea of what awaited them that December day.

By shortly after 10 A.M., the men—and some boys who were not yet in their teens—were hard at work deep underground in the Monongah coal mines. Suddenly a violent explosion tore through the mines. The earth shook for miles around. People above ground stumbled and fell. A streetcar was thrown from its rails. At one mine entrance, a string of runaway mining cars crashed, blocking the opening. At another entrance, the blast destroyed the mine's mechanical system and tore open the surface of the ground.

A stray spark or flame probably touched off the explosion of methane gas and coal dust. Underground, the fierce blast raced through the dark tunnels. It caused countless cave-ins and a fire that gave off intense heat,

After the explosion, people gathered around the blocked entrance to mine No. 8.

thick smoke, and poisonous gases. The explosion shattered hundreds of lives forever.

More than 360 men and boys were killed. They left behind wives and mothers and children. Today the Monongah mining explosion remains the worst mining disaster in the history of the United States.

A Sleepy Town

Monongah is tucked in the rolling foothills of the Appalachian Mountains in northern West Virginia. It was a mining town from its earliest days. Laid out in 1850, the area was first called Briar Town and had no post office. When Monongahela Coal and Coke moved in, the company established mines and a processing plant. It also opened a post office and company store. In 1891, Briar Town became Monongahela, but it was soon shortened to Monongah.

The mines later became part of the Fairmont Coal Company. In 1903, Consolidation Coal Company bought a majority of Fairmont and became the controlling stockholder. As a result, Monongah mines were part of the largest mining company in the United States.

The company made a great deal of money by mining coal from deep underground. Coal forms when organic material—leaves, plants, and trees—is squeezed under enormous pressure and heat. Over millions of years that

The Fairmont Coal Company began with a mine near Fairmont, West Virginia. As the mine grew more successful, the company expanded.

organic matter turns into coal. When coal is burned, it creates heat to make steam that drives locomotives, powers industrial machinery, and heats homes. Today coal is mostly used to drive steam turbines that create electricity.

Getting to the coal is never easy, and 100 years ago it was even harder and more dangerous. In the Monongah mines, deep tunnels had to be dug in the earth to reach the coal. Miners drilled into the earth, placed explosives deep in the holes, and blasted the coal away in large chunks. The men then loaded the coal onto trains of special coal cars and brought it to the surface.

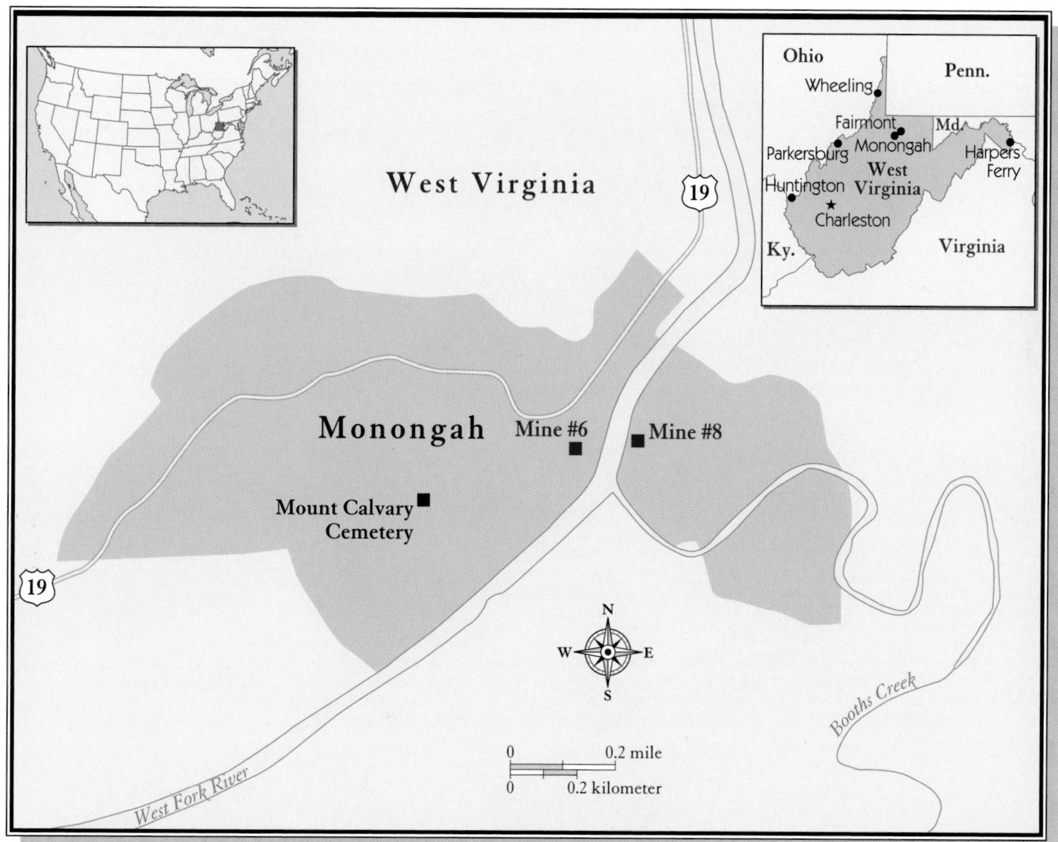

Monongah was a small town located close to the larger city of Fairmont.

In the early 1900s, the Monongah mines were among the most advanced in the industry. They were connected underground, which was a modern feature. Electricity was used to help remove the coal. Locomotives were used to haul it along the main tunnels underground and at the surface. And a series of large,

In mines where electricity was used, the power lines ran close to the miners' heads.

mechanical fans helped bring fresh air into the largest sections of the mines.

The Monongah mines were worked in the Pittsburgh seam. This large and long deposit of coal produced huge amounts of the rich, black mineral. There was also a large amount of methane gas in the mines. The combination of this highly flammable gas, coal, and dust meant even the smallest spark could turn deadly. Fires and explosions were always a risk.

For the miners, it was dark and dangerous work. In addition to the explosion risks, digging coal created a fine dust that caked miners' faces, clogged their noses, and choked their lungs. For many, though, the risks were worth even the meager pay they received. At the time of the accident, the average pay for a miner in West Virginia came out to 75 cents for a 10-hour day, although pay rates and daily schedules varied. But coal mining positions were among the only jobs to be had in West Virginia.

Some of the workers were just boys—10, 11,

Trapper boys spent most of their 10-hour workdays waiting to open the ventilation doors for coal cars.

and 12 years old. Most of the younger boys worked as "trappers." They were responsible for opening and closing ventilation doors so coal cars could pass through the mine tunnels. Older boys with more experience often became mule drivers. They led mules as the animals pulled coal cars through the mines. The oldest boys who learned the craft became coal loaders. They were often assigned to work alongside their relatives.

At the time of the disaster, Monongah had about 3,000 residents. Almost everybody who lived in Monongah either worked in the mines or was related to somebody who did. Most of the other jobs in town were there to provide goods or services to the miners.

Before the disaster, Monongah had a hotel and a trolley car line that served several nearby cities. Downtown Monongah was a lively center, with several restaurants, saloons, and grocery stores. And there was

When photographers came to record the work of miners, young boys feared they were going to be forced to go to school.

Some Monongah residents could view the destruction at mine No. 6 from their hilltop homes.

a "company store" where miners could convert their paychecks directly into goods.

Monongah was home to a large number of recent immigrants, families that had moved to the United States from other countries. Many of them came from Italy, seeking a better life and higher wages. While there were many

The Monongah Mining Disaster • The Monongah Mining Disaster • The Monongah

American-born people among the dead, other victims came from Greece, Poland, Hungary, and a number of other European countries.

Many of Monongah's houses were built on the hillsides above the mines. Most of these modest homes housed miners and their families. When the explosion struck that fateful morning, those tiny homes shook. Women and children waiting for their husbands, sons, and brothers to come home from the mines knew something was terribly wrong.

MOVING TO ACTION

A full shift of miners had set to work that December day shortly after 10 A.M. The explosion that rocked the mines and shook the earth occurred at 10:28. Those above the

Broken timbers and wrecked cars blocked the entrance into mine No. 8.

ground knew the tremors could mean only one thing.

Women grabbed their children. Along with the few men remaining in the town, they rushed to the mine entrance. What they found was discouraging. At the main entrance to mine No. 6, a string of ore cars had broken loose and plunged back into the mine, crashing at the bottom of the slope. The entrance to mine No. 8 was destroyed. The dirt banks surrounding the opening had collapsed all around it.

Without immediate access to the mines, nobody could guess the extent of the catastrophe. They did not know whether the mine was engulfed in flames or choked with poisonous gas. Some mining officials gathered in small groups to begin venturing into the mines. Other officials were busy clearing surface wreckage at mine No. 8. With little information about the fate of their loved ones, women began screaming and children started crying. The few remaining men on the surface geared up for the rescue.

Fairmont Coal's general manager tried to bring

Townspeople were asked to stay back from the mine opening. Many watched from the hillside.

order to the chaos. He put together a security team to keep onlookers at a distance and organized a rescue team. About 20 minutes after the blast, the mine's general superintendent, a mine foreman, a fire boss, and a crew of carpenters entered mine No. 6 to begin the search for survivors. They discovered the first victims at the slope at the bottom of the entrance, where the ore cars had crashed.

But there was some hope. Shortly after the explosion, four miners emerged. They had escaped through a small opening in the earth. At first, they had tried crawling out by feeling along the rails of the main entrance. However, the smoke became too thick, and they had to turn back.

One of the men recalled seeing a crack in the mine a few days earlier, so the group sought out the opening. One man was injured, and the others had to help him along. They found the narrow crack and worked together to boost a man through it. He pulled himself to daylight. Rescuers on the outside rushed to help the others. Bloody, dazed, and confused, the four survivors knew nothing about the victims still trapped below, nor did they know the condition of the mines.

A Maze of Mayhem

The explosion caused vast damage throughout the mines. Earth and rock caved in around the underground entrance to mine No. 8. Tight tunnels were transformed into a mass

Rescue workers had to clear the cave-in at the No. 8 entrance before they could enter the mine.

of twisted metal, splintered wood, and heavy rock. The explosion wrecked the ventilation system that helped supply air to the miners. Massive fans were knocked out of service.

As word of the explosion spread, volunteers eager to help continued to gather at the site. But the lack of fresh air not only put the miners in danger, it also put would-be rescuers at risk. Fumes from the toxic gases were powerful. Rescuers could work underground for just 15 minutes before being forced to surface for fresh air. A few of them had to be rescued themselves. Those who stayed below too long were seriously hurt by the gases. They had to be taken away for treatment.

Rescuers were forced to work in relay shifts. This method slowed their progress in getting to any survivors. Wreckage blocked many of the tunnels, adding to delays. Rescue workers had to clear the debris before they could move forward.

Hope for the trapped miners diminished with every passing minute. If the powerful fumes were preventing

Though rescue workers did not want to stop and take breaks, failing to do so would have put their health in danger.

rescuers from spending more than 15 minutes in the caves, what chance did a miner deep underground have?

In a fully functioning mine, structures called brattices and overcasts are used to create spaces that direct fresh air through the mines. The structures make passageways for fumes to escape and fresh air to enter. A large explosion in a mine destroys brattices and overcasts. The ventilation system is destroyed and piles of bricks are left in its place.

Without a reliable fresh-air system, rescuers were forced to improvise. They had a smaller fan that was still working. They positioned it near a small opening. As they made their way through the tunnels, recovery workers set up two wooden posts, then nailed boards across the top and bottom. This created a rough frame. The team then stretched rolled canvas across the frame.

A second crew followed and put boards over the entire structure. A third crew came behind them to fill in any cracks with concrete and mortar to make it airtight. The structure directed fresh outside air through the tunnels while blocking dust. The rescuers made their way to the lower levels of the mine.

But as they went deeper, they found more obstacles.

The Monongah Mining Disaster • The Monongah Mining Disaster • The Monongah

Choking coal dust, piles of rubble, and a tangle of wrecked equipment slowed their progress and sapped their strength. The rescue teams were making little progress.

Although the fires were out, the heat was unbearable. Afterdamp—a mix of gases that hangs in the air after an explosion—was heavy in some parts of the mine. It made volunteers nauseous and gave them headaches. After hours of searching, they found body after body. The smell of death was overwhelming. Yet the search did not stop. Rescuers held out hope that there were at least some workers still alive deep in the corners of the mine.

At 4 P.M., a few hours after the first survivors had emerged, there was another glimmer of hope. Moaning echoed through a narrow hole near the surface. A rope was dangled through the opening. A rescuer was lowered 100 feet (30.5 meters) into the mine. There he found miner Peter Urban sitting on the body of his dead brother Stanislaus.

In mining accidents such as Monongah, victims were often buried under debris, and bodies had to be dug out.

Peter stared bleary-eyed into space, stunned by the shock of all that had happened. He was so upset and confused he even fought against rescuers who tried to get

Peter Urban was the only person to be rescued, and he is often called the sole survivor of the Monongah mining disaster. However, four other men also survived by escaping on their own.

him out. Finally, he was overpowered and brought to the surface. As it would turn out, he was the last survivor of the Monongah disaster.

Rescue Becomes a Recovery Effort

Families remained gathered at the entrances to the two mines. They prayed for any information about their loved ones below. But rescue efforts continued with little encouraging news.

Many of the miners' wives held young children in their arms as they sat waiting for news.

Many of the bodies that were brought to the surface were badly mangled and burned. Town officials set up a temporary morgue in a partially constructed bank building nearby. They stored the bodies there until they were claimed and funeral arrangements were made. Because the bodies were in terrible shape, identifying victims was a challenge.

Miners were supposed to carry numbered brass tags that would help identify them in case of a fire. These tags had a corresponding tag on a board near the mine entrances. But at least one of those boards had been destroyed in the explosion. Many of the dead had to be identified based on their clothing or personal possessions. Some of them—particularly the youngest workers—were never identified. Families argued over the identities of the dead. On more than one occasion, two families laid claim to a single body.

A newspaper article dated December 8, 1907, illustrated the scene that unfolded as the dead were brought back to town:

Caskets were hauled to the mines. The bodies were then safely transported to the temporary morgue.

"The rapidity with which the remains began to be recovered … necessitated the coal company pressing into service a number of transfer wagons. These were filled with straw and the gruesome work of carting the charred remains across the river through the dense crowd began. … The weeping of the bereaved ones as they madly chimed after the vehicles was heartrending. They overwhelmed the morgue in their clamors for a look at the dead and it was necessary to drive them back by force and draw ropes across the main street."

By December 10, four days after the explosion, it was clear that Peter Urban would be the only man rescued from the Monongah disaster. Relatives of those missing were still hoping for a miracle. But that miracle never came.

Families waited on Monongah's main street for their loved ones' bodies.

The entire mine was infused with fresh air by December 12, and searchers had recovered 337 bodies. Another 25 bodies were discovered during the final cleanup efforts. One of them was not even a mine employee. He was an insurance salesman who had gone underground to meet with potential customers.

There were not enough caskets in Monongah for all the casualties. Coffins were brought in from surrounding towns, but those quickly ran out, too. An undertaker ordered 100 coffins to be delivered from Zanesville, Ohio. Other orders followed. Hundreds of plain wooden boxes lined the streets of downtown. Embalmers worked around the clock to care for the dead.

In order to handle all of the services, churches conducted funerals several times a day. On nearby hillsides, dozens of men teamed up to dig long rows of graves.

When the final tally was made, 362 men and boys had lost their lives in the Monongah mine explosion. About 250 wives and more than 1,000 children were left

A new graveyard was created for the victims of the mining disaster.

without any means of support.

The people of West Virginia heeded calls for clothing and money. Some took widows and orphans into their homes. But for most of those left behind, the future was bleak. They were penniless and hungry. Grim reminders of the tragedy were never far away. Row upon row of fresh graves were dug in the hillside near their homes. And a steady stream of horse-drawn wagons delivered new caskets for days.

In mid-January, the Marion County coroner's jury sought to determine the cause of the Monongah explosion.

The jury made several safety recommendations in its report, including hiring additional mining inspectors for the region.

The jury concluded that it was caused by the ignition of methane gas. The gas explosion then caused the highly flammable coal dust to explode. It shook the earth and turned the mines into flaming tombs of wreckage. The jury found the ignition itself could have come from runaway coal cars or from an improperly fired blast into the coal.

Exactly what lit the methane gas remains a mystery. Experts have argued a variety of theories. It could have been carelessness with an open flame in a lamp, a blast gone wrong, or a stray spark from some electrical equipment. Whatever the cause, it was clear there were a number of dangerous conditions in place.

REFORMS AMID THE FALLOUT

The Monongah disaster was just the first in a string of accidents in the mining industry. From 1907 to 1909, more than 1,200 miners died in mining accidents in West Virginia alone. There were explosions and cave-ins. By 1910, 2,600 miners were dying each year in mines across the country.

Less than a year after the Monongah disaster, more than 150 miners died in an accident in Marianna, Pennsylvania.

The tragedies forced the U.S. government to confront the growing safety concerns. Less than two weeks after the Monongah accident, the federal government issued a report on mining deaths and accidents. The report blamed a general lack of information about the explosives being used in mining. It claimed those men working with explosives were not always trained to handle them properly. Officials also pointed to a decline in European mining deaths. They said the decrease was the result of increased governmental regulations.

By 1908, coal mine companies began to take notice. They realized that dangerous mines were expensive and unproductive. The following year, a mining business journal reported that a lack of safety precautions decreased profits. The journal suggested that companies adopting strict safety measures would be more profitable.

At the same time, a growing political movement was taking aim at the mining industry. The Progressives pressed for new laws to improve mining conditions. Meanwhile, mining officials were rushing to adopt regulations of their own. They hoped to avoid any government intrusion on their industry.

But the death toll was too high for the government not to get involved. In 1910, Congress established the U.S. Bureau of Mines. As a part of the Department of the Interior, the new bureau was to research mine safety,

Safety equipment was developed in response to the accidents of the early 1900s. A new mine rescue car was equipped with items for mine emergencies.

Despite the forming of the Bureau of Mines, mining remained a high-risk job.

investigate accidents, and inspect mines, with the aim of preventing more tragedies. The bureau's orders were clear, but its powers were minimal. Mining companies had to let inspectors into the mines. But the bureau was not given the authority to force companies to follow their recommendations. There was little improvement in mine safety.

Mining Today and Tomorrow

Eventually, stricter safety regulations were put in place. But mining remains a dangerous job. When disaster strikes deep underground, there are often few places to hide or escape. Poisonous gases, explosions, and cave-ins are constant threats.

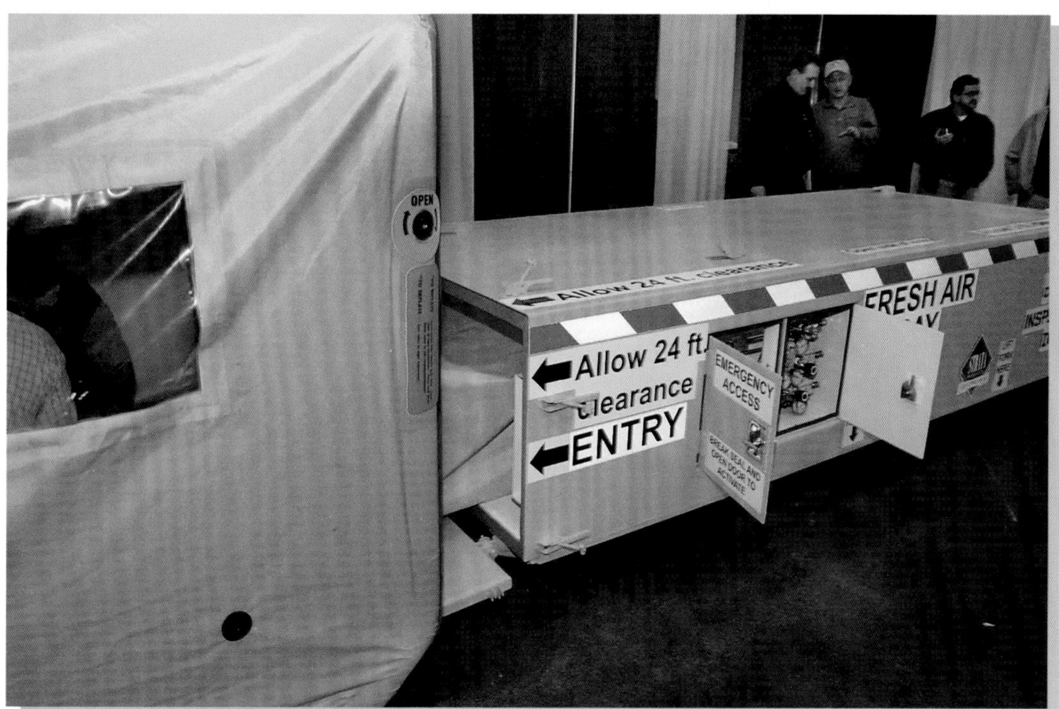

New technology helps make the mining industry safer. A portable fresh-air bay is designed to provide a safe area for stranded miners.

Modern mining operations have become more automated and safer. Machines are more often used in place of people. Some companies are working to develop robots that could venture deep into mines with cameras and equipment to detect dangerous gases. Workers are regularly trained on the latest safety measures such as escape routes and rescue breathing devices. Some of the most modern mines use boreholes, secured chambers with thick walls and a supply of fresh air. These areas can keep workers alive in case of fire or a gas leak.

Mining operations in the Monongah area continue to this day. But 100 years after the worst mining disaster in U.S. history, Monongah does not look like the city that suffered such a great loss so long ago. It is a quiet town of about 900 people, one elementary school, and one middle school. Crime is low, and the downtown struggles to survive.

In 2007, a statue was erected near the Town Hall of Monongah as a tribute to the women whose husbands and sons died in the 1907 disaster. The granite statue depicts a

The statue was dedicated at a ceremony in August 2007.

woman cradling a baby boy in one arm. Her other arm is draped around a small girl at her side. Some people refer to it as the "Madonna of Monongah," in reference to Mary, the mother of Jesus Christ. It serves as a reminder of the sacrifices of the people of Monongah.

Glossary

embalmers—people who preserve a body for a funeral

improvise—to make or use whatever is at hand

infused—filled with

methane—a colorless, odorless gas that is highly flammable

nauseous—to feel sick to one's stomach

organic materials—items that are obtained from something once living and that contain the element carbon

Progressives—members of a political movement that sought economic, political, and social reform; the Progressive era lasted from about 1890 to 1920

tremors—the shaking of the ground usually associated with earthquakes

ventilation—a system or means of providing fresh air

Did You Know?

- In 2005, 23 workers were killed in U.S. mines—the fewest number of mining deaths in U.S. history.
- The year 1907 was the worst year for mining fatalities in the United States, when 3,242 miners were killed on the job.
- After the Monongah accident, the Consolidation Coal Company gave $17,500 to a relief fund and later gave an additional small settlement to individual survivors.
- In a strange twist of fate, Peter Urban was killed nearly two decades later in the same mine where he was rescued. A section of slate broke loose from the roof above him, crushing him to death.

Important Dates

Timeline

1891 The town of Monongah, West Virginia, is founded.

1907 On December 6, the Monongah mining disaster kills 362 men and boys.

1910 The U.S. Congress establishes the U.S. Bureau of Mines to develop and enforce new mining safety laws.

1952 Congress passes the Federal Coal Mine Safety Act, requiring the annual inspection of certain underground mines and empowering the government to fine mining companies for violations.

1969 The Federal Coal Mine Health and Safety Act is adopted, toughening safety and health standards and strengthening the government's enforcement powers.

2006 On January 2, an explosion at the Sago, West Virginia, mine kills 12 men.

2007 On August 6, a mine collapse in Utah kills six miners; three rescue workers are killed in a second collapse on August 16.

Important People

Clarence Wayland Watson (1864–1940)

One of the founders of the Fairmont Coal Company, Watson was central to the merger of Fairmont Coal and the Consolidation Coal Company; at the time of the merger he was named president of Consolidation Coal; he served in the U.S. Senate from 1911 to 1913, filling a vacancy left after a senator died

E.S. Amos (?-?)

The county coroner in charge of identifying the bodies of the victims; he was also the elected justice of the peace who served as chairman of the investigation into the cause of the fatal explosion

Peter Urban (?-1925?)

The only person rescued from the mines; emigrated from Austria in 1891 and lived in one of the homes owned by the mining company; though still shaken at the time of the investigation, Urban testified before the coroner's jury

Want to Know More?

More Books to Read

Bartoletti, Susan Campbell. *Growing Up in Coal Country*. Boston: Houghton Mifflin Co., 1996.

Di Piazza, Domenica. *West Virginia*. Minneapolis: Lerner Publications, 2002.

Easton, Richard. *A Real American.* New York: Clarion Books, 2002.

Edwards, Ron, and Adrianna Edwards. *Coal.* New York: Crabtree Publishing Company, 2004.

Hughes, Pat. *The Breaker Boys*. New York: Farrar, Straus and Giroux, 2004.

Kalman, Bobbie, and Kate Calder. *The Life of a Miner.* New York: Crabtree Publishing Company, 2000.

On the Web

For more information on this topic, use FactHound.

1. Go to *www.facthound.com*
2. Type in this book ID: 0756535131
3. Click on the *Fetch It* button.

FactHound will find the best Web sites for you.

On the Road

Beckley Exhibition Coal Mine
513 Ewart Ave.
Beckley, WV 25801
304/256-1747
A youth museum that offers a look at what mines were like in the early 1900s

Town of Pocahontas Exhibition Coal Mine and Museum
Centre Street
Pocahontas, VA 24635-0128
276/945-2134
Guided tours of the Pocahontas Exhibition Coal Mine

Look for more We the People books about this era:

The American Newsboy
Angel Island
The Great Chicago Fire
Great Women of the Suffrage Movement
The Harlem Renaissance
The Haymarket Square Tragedy
The Hindenburg
Industrial America
The Johnstown Flood
The Klondike Gold Rush
The Lowell Mill Girls
The Orphan Trains
The Pullman Strike of 1894
Roosevelt's Rough Riders
The Triangle Shirtwaist Factory Fire
Women of the Harlem Renaissance
Yellow Journalism

A complete list of We the People titles is available on our Web site: www.compasspointbooks.com

The Monongah Mining Disaster • The Monongah Mining Disaster • The Monongah

Index

About the Author

Jason Skog is a writer who lives in Brooklyn, New York, with his wife and son. He has been a newspaper writer for 11 years, covering education, courts, police, government, and youth issues. His work has appeared in magazines and newspapers, including *The New York Times*, *Boston Globe*, and *Baltimore Sun*. He is a member of the Society of Children's Book Writers and Illustrators, and he has written several books for young readers.